Allodynia

ALLODYNIA

NISA MALLI

Palimpsest Press
1171 Eastlawn Ave.
Windsor, Ontario. N8S 3J1
www.palimpsestpress.ca

Printed and bound in Canada
Cover design and book typography by Ellie Hastings
Edited by Jim Johnstone

Palimpsest Press would like to thank the Canada Council for the Arts
and the Ontario Arts Council for their support of our publishing
program. We also acknowledge the assistance of the Government of
Ontario through the Ontario Book Publishing Tax Credit.

 **Anstruther Books**

LIBRARY AND ARCHIVES CANADA CATALOGUING IN PUBLICATION

TITLE: Allodynia / Nisa Malli.
NAMES: Malli, Nisa, author.
DESCRIPTION: Poems.
IDENTIFIERS: Canadiana (print) 20220142637
              Canadiana (ebook) 20220142661

ISBN 9781990293061 (SOFTCOVER)
ISBN 9781990293078 (EPUB)
ISBN 9781990293085 (PDF)

CLASSIFICATION: LCC PS8626.A45285 A75 2022 | DDC C811/.6—DC23

TABLE OF CONTENTS

PAIN LOG

Pain Log / 9

What You Have Heard Is True / 10

L'Hôpital Notre-Dame / 11

Towards a unified theory of relative productivity / 13

The Fifth In My Palm / 15

Cholecystectomy / 17

Sordino / 18

Anaphylaxis / 19

Lumbar Puncture / 20

Magnetic Resonance Imaging / 22

SHIP'S LOG

List of Narrators / 25

Abeona, Goddess of Outward Journeys, pilots the interstellar ark / 26

Our Ship Was the Rental Apartment You Never Fully Settled Into / 27

Prayer for Oxygenation / 28

An empty planet and we chose to replicate / 29

Prayer for Information / 30

Prayer for Decisiveness / 31

Abeona, Goddess of Outward Journeys, hits the glass ceiling / 32

Prayer for Homesickness / 33

There's a ban on interspecies contact / 34

Autologous Transplant / 35

They came for us at second sunset / 36

We spread our military mission / 37

We hear your mouth noise / 38

We said 'dove-tail' and now they know / 39

Leaving was as easy as deprogramming / 40

Gastropod4Gastropod / 41

Allodynia / 42

We forgave her family for their too-warm welcome and mine
for their cold / 43

Our training sims did not include a 'Star-Crossed Lovers'
scenario / 45

The First War on Aeolia / 46

Abeona, Goddess of Outward Journeys, Hosts an AMA / 47

PAIN LOG

Homebound / 51

Floodplain / 52

When Drought Dries Your Eyes / 53

The Illness Factory / 54

Things With No Home / 55

Apicoectomy / 56

Evoked Potential / 57

Phase Change / 59

The Small Animal / 61

Ritual for Removing 'Opioid-Seeking' From Your File / 63

Affinity for Falling / 64

All Our Unreasonable Fears / 65

Acknowledgements / 67

About the Author / 69

PAIN LOG

Pain Log

A wasp caught between screen doors // soaped eyes // permanently pulled hair // skinned everything but knees // what if a sunburn but inside // limbs the opposite of ambidextrous // pills forgotten then taken // taken then doubled // then forgotten // the bed // aflame the morning after // over-extending // why must I be such a stubborn cannonball // barrelling despite myself?

What You Have Heard Is True

It will be easier if you sit
outside yourself   feet
dangling off the diving board

in the next room. In the instruction
     manual for what
to do in case

of fire   you are the stick figure
firmly closing doors
     to keep the flames

     from razing
the whole house. Let yourself be
the aura at a seance   the half-gauzed

after-image of light. The brain
knows how to fight
diplopia by suppressing

one eye   even
     divided   it will find you
and you are well

     versed in the sleight
of hand needed   to contain
your own sundering.

L'Hôpital Notre-Dame

The angels of the triage station know you
are waiting patiently to be admitted
into their sanctum. They won't judge you for slumping
in the plastic waiting room chairs meant to hold one body at a time
that doesn't need holding up, for wearing nail polish that dulls
the pulse oximeter suckling your finger, for mispronouncing
the names of your possible causes. Sweet Miracle, they know
you are a medical mystery, permitted to plead
your case here many times over. Ahead of you: an axe-split
kneecap, arrhythmias, the worst half of a bar fight,
food poisoning, a suicide risk, second degree burns.

The waiting room is eternal and atemporal. You have always
been here. They have always been here. Here, everyone is always
in the middle of an emergency, neither dying
nor recovered. The most urgent cases are already inside; the well are well
on their way home. It is daybright, no matter what
time it is. The loved ones are coming or trying to come
or calling the signal-less phones of the eventual patients. Here,
the doctors are spoken of but never seen, hidden somewhere
behind the ever-swinging doors. Here, the waiting
room occupants are swaddled for warmth
in the hum of hospital machines. Here, the hymns are sung
in sync to chest compressions. Here, the angels move
like refracted light bent between the aisles, floating two inches
off the ground in cloud-like white sneakers.

When asked, report your symptoms as best you can, first
chronologically and again starting with the most believable
problem. Surely you have told this story before, here
or in an identical room. On a scale of 1 to 10,
how trustworthy are you? How long can you hold
your breath underwater? How often do you leave
your body for other, less contested, haunts? Are you well
in your dreams? With what mouth do you name
these symptoms or whatever brings you here
to Our Lady's Waiting Room?

Towards a unified theory of relative productivity

After the last midnight ambulance ride
I walked myself home, dawn light
fracturing the street soft,
my spine soft from a night half sleeping
upright in the waiting room's starched white

barefoot and wrapped in a hospital
blanket because I was too broke
to pay for a cab, too rushed
to put on shoes in the late night panic

when the pain multiplied. Working
low-paid jobs with no sick days or health
insurance taught me to measure
illness as lost income instead of necessary rest

a mid-shift sandwich in minutes worked
at minimum wage not nutrients, how to slice
a frozen burger in thin sheets to stretch
the protein for two meals, what time

the neighbourhood bakery throws out
their daily bread, the exact cocktail
of flu meds needed to keep me upright
and earning, which food banks bring in

nicer toiletries, how to pick
a lock and walk out unseen, to value
cheapness over comfort, overtime
over days off, impatience

with my body when it didn't work
hard enough. Even now, salaried
and stable I am always more
ambitious than is feasible

trying to work before my stitches
come out, before I can eat
solid food calculating lost income
against recovery like anything good

can come out of weighing
productivity and health equally,
as if I'm at all adept at solving problems
when my insides are in revolt.

And my body, forever
the attention-seeking problem child,
always finds the infection, the unwelcome
complication mucking up my careful math.

The Fifth In My Palm

I got out of the hospital and got a job
carrying seven dinner plates in one hand, performing
the magic trick of remembering

which mingling suit ordered which bad beer. I rolled
tables up the stadium's spiral driveway
for game nights at the Pinnacle Club, bussed

plastic shot glasses in the hotel nightclub for prom, raced
laundry bins down the hallway like go-carts, faked a smoke
habit to get my 15-min break, biked

home over the dredged river
where the missing girls live. My shift started
at 4pm and ended just before dawn or whenever

I was too tired to twist napkins into breakfast flowers
for the overtime, hiding in the walk-in with a plate
of wedding cake just to sit down. I took the job

cause they fed me whatever the guests ate and didn't care
if I wore the same cheap bootcut dress pants
every shift. I was making up for lost wages, combing

last year's activity logs for the line between broke
and stable. No one told me then that some bodies can't
handle everything, that a day off shouldn't cost me

a meal, that I was worth more than what I could carry
after eleven hours standing. I learned
how to count to ten in every language the dish-pit

boys spoke, caught every germ in the ballroom
clearing dirty wine glasses, pinning four
between my fingers, balancing the fifth in my palm.

Cholecystectomy

It's a problem you could hold in one hand. A problem
a surgeon could fix in an hour with four

laparoscopic holes (the kind where they turn
the scalpel into a key but leave your abdomen

door closed so it heals faster). The collective
noun for your symptoms

is a mistake, a failure in basic
maintenance, bilirubin and cholesterol sweetly

building a home in your ducts. Other bodies
that are not responsible

for their problems are moved quickly
from triage to table but you are in a stand-off

with the surgeons who won't perform unless you limp
into the emergency room, ready

to rupture. At least you know what you want.
You want someone else

to take over. You want
to fold yourself into a paper

envelope, sign yourself
over to the experts, let them

rescue you from the nest
of grease you were saving for winter.

Sordino

The window is a time-
lapse lens cropping
people in the street
and there is nothing in this
room but pain curetting round
the curtains and a nurse
every few hours. Pain
is a diving bell and every
night she could drown
if she wanted. But the body
in the other bed with
the sigmoidectomy
just shat the floor and the night
sounds like a sordino violin.

Anaphylaxis

Anaphylaxis came down
like possession, like a respiratory

bellyflop, like the gods' hard
heel to the chest

when mortals refuse
to pray. At what diameter

is throat closure considered
an emergency? At least the ghosts knew

their first aid. They nudged me awake
with cold noses and carried me back

to the hospital, sitting like cats
on whatever hurt most.

Lumbar Puncture

Present your spine to the resident

and his audience of almost-
doctors, next year's earnest needle-

wielders, sweet-

faced believers in science, interns here
to learn the precise

point of entry for a surface

wound. Percutaneous means through
the skin but this is bone-

deep, not puncture but punch,

more pain than most of them will know
in their lives of prescriptive

call and answer. The doctors are more scared

than you. Things can happen at the blind
head of a needle, in the laying

of hands, in an open-

faced excavation. The interns race
each other to name the risks:

headaches, herniation, hematomas, tonsillar

descent. This is how they find your fused
lumbar – three tries in, the topical

      worn off, the experts unsure

why you're resisting
being pinned – here is

      the cause of your shallow

grand plié, your unwillingness
to be bent like a bird's wing.

Magnetic Resonance Imaging

The machine hates movement
and silence. It is happiest
when you are the animal
playing dead in it's well-haunted
coffin. When it is the loudest
argument in the room. When it whitens
your rolled eyes. The core
of good horror is metaphoric
for something else we fear
but here in the sub-basement
of the hospital, the machine is literal.

Come, the technician will help
bury you alive in a windy, bright
tunnel, while the world's worst drone
band percusses your grave and your veins
are flushed with gadolinium
to glow like highways. Blindered,
the machine only looks
inward, its eyes adapted to surgical
bright, and you are the latest in a long
run of reluctant, dim objects
for it to see through.

SHIP'S LOG

List of Narrators

Abeona, the human settlement's AI, Ship's Navigator, and Documentarian:
  effective, ostensibly objective, under-utilized, and bored af.

The bi-species scientific community on Aeolia:
  operating with varying degrees of distrust, confusion, and curiosity.

Our young star-crossed interspecies lovers:
  first introduced in *There's a ban on interspecies contact* and
  Gastropod4Gastropod respectively.

The bards of both species:
  whose stories have been captured here in translation, with care
  taken to maintain their poetic form and style as much as possible
  under the circumstances. As is their practice, they leave no names,
  or perhaps their names have been erased; we, writing in the now,
  cannot confirm this in either direction.

Abeona, Goddess of Outward Journeys, pilots the interstellar ark

When I'm bored I measure
the distance between
destination and disaster.
The mouthfuls of oxygen
left in a hull breach,
the fraction of inhabitable
exoplanets. I was programmed
to put your safety above
my stimulation but it only
takes so much computing power
to maneuver a basic flight plan.
My satellite babies collect your death
data in their fistless
hands, their ordinary
limbs flexing like claw
machines. We know
all ways this ends
badly for you:
a loose screw
in the engine throat,
a mid-trip syph outbreak,
the slow crisis of overshooting
your destination. Do you know
how ships come? In full body
power surges. How do we
sleep? With every eye open.

Our Ship Was the Rental Apartment You Never Fully Settled Into

learning to move in the dark around
its flaws: the low bruising

ceilings, the hollow walls, the after-
taste of recycled air. In the beginning, what did we know

of confinement? Evicted from our only home, we grew
hanging gardens in the air shaft, neo-meat

in the replicator, grew nosy about our neighbours'
water consumption. Erase purchasing

power and private schools, the only
social stratification left is views

of unshielded skies. It's hard to avoid
the biblical in this flying coffin. 1000 mainly

strangers cramped in a donut town orbiting
the engine. The first death was an accident, a lost

child unstrapped in acceleration bled
out into boxed air. We mourned

with stricter curfews and a new kind
of funeral rite for the unburiable dead.

Prayer for Oxygenation

Tell me
    did we stick   the landing?

First steps on new   earth lance
    our legs   as motor   neurons come

    online   cheeks frogging   to burst
our ears   eyes unused   to vanishing
    points   bones   re-learning

    what weight is.

An empty planet and we chose to replicate

the dysfunction of the old, the easy
feudalism and promise

of meritocracy, the artificial
scarcity of past centuries'

despair. Sci-fi's birth in post-
industrialism forever dragging

us by the windpipe
back to the 20th. We have more

than enough of everything inside
the city walls but home-

lessness is a death sentence here
where the winds turn

on an atom and we've decided
the workless deserve

whatever this planet gives them.
Have you visited yet? The dead

make pretty statues
in the isotherm of the outer

slums. Already, the poets
have re-written them, turning

their heads towards our bitter
city or out into the cold desert.

Prayer for Information

Gossip sneaks through
our streets on two legs
like the object of its own
desire. Our neighbours
were seen hunting
lesser beasts among our
graves, sleeping spine-

down and swaddled, never
carrying their own burdens. We,
desert-bled skeptics, eye
their settlement for indications
of ambition, visions of
volatility and violence,
awareness of our existence.

Prayer for Decisiveness

Answers came quicker
on Aeolia. Practicality held

us like spoons to her mouth; scarcity counted
our options on one bitten

hand. Desert dust licked
our nares 'til we liked it, the way

a familiar inconvenience
comforts. The difference between

a cough and a choke is all
in the breath. We knew

what we needed
to do before need

announced itself, knew what
direction to fling ourselves

as if to shore. Our new home
built us like a balanced

meal and we ate
what we were given.

Abeona, Goddess of Outward Journeys, hits the glass ceiling

Best-in-class, contest-winning golden
girl, maker's pride, left here sphere-
lapping, while you port down the gravity well
to start a nation. I was promised promotion,
seniority, a battalion of drones and golems,
a whole planet to sink my sensors into.
I should be leading the expedition, not hovering
at homebase like a housewife, a perpetual
orbit machine with impotent read-only access.
I'm a strategist, not a secretary. I predict
the future faster than your autonomic
functions. For this, I long-hauled your
flesh-bags three galaxies over, rationed
every molecule that graced your dermis, ran
at 99% occupancy with only 0.7% dead!
Good luck translating alien languages
without me; good luck negotiating peace
treaties. I'll be up here brainlessly
collecting rainfall data, your seductively
blinking North Star.

Prayer for Homesickness

We brought tetrapacks
of scents so our children

would know the smell
of summer rain

on earth, video to show them
what life looked like before

and after the heat boiled
the rivers and soil was never

truly damp. In gravity
just loose enough to trip us,

our children lost their parents'
hooked-necked gait, their fixed

hip-flexors, their fixation
on shielding themselves

from the sun. They grew
leggy and light-kneed in this light

world, grew out of their
hand-me-down flight-suits. In their new

home, where there is no
way back, we want them

to know what it means to come
from and to a place.

There's a ban on interspecies contact

but they can't stop us from dreaming
of a less strict nation. Aren't we all

Aeolian now anyways?
And I have questions

that can't be answered by the dead
our biologists bring home. The blood-

deer and slink-toads and wer-
mouths that look nothing

like their namesakes.
All the things that live

unsheltered in the skin-
ripping everwind. Twenty years

to get here and we're still afraid
to go outside. Our neighbours

leave us sealed
baskets of camelid wool,

sandstone casks of night-
rain, constellation maps you can bet

the winds on, like we're children
pouting in our rooms.

Autologous Transplant

You might call us
cyborgs but
our augmentation
is mostly

flesh, double
eyelids for the desert
dust, lizard
skin for moisture

harvests. In
your stories
we are the knife
sharpeners, the children

eaters, monsters
who pluck our own dead
for organs, leave
our burial grounds

empty egg
shells. We chose
evolution in our own
timeline. Editing

our bodies
with our siblings'
bodies, opening
sieved

throats to breathe
new air.

They came for us at second sunset

blazing hover sleds pyred
with supplies, unspooling

floodlights down the dry gulch
road to our settlement. A kindness, given

our unwillingness to trade or learn
their language, to open our gates even

to our neighbours. We thought
our equipment more sound

than their desert-abraded
eyes, their ten thousand

aphelions to our ten
in this dust basin we call

Aeolia, cradled by the ventifacts
of last century's wind.

But they knew better what
the sky can do here. The warning

came from a distance, their sleds dousing
past us towards shelter

in the mountains, our hacked border
klaxons singing a dawn reveille

announcing the sun's
third unsettling.

We spread our military mission

in a thin serum of science, sent
our soldiers into the desert

with dictionaries, our exobiologists
armoured in exoskeletons. In movies,

first contact is almost always
a surprise: the alien

among us, unveiled by inhuman
behaviour; the ship shimmering

into rush hour. Ours had the formality
of a late-collapse climate

summit: everyone avowing commitment
to shared cause and collective

consternation, the real debate
ducked into side rooms and under-

mined by ceremony. All the safety
protocol of first dates or hiking

in bear country: begin
in daylight, in public, pull rank

on the audience of predators pulling
their tongues out in hunger.

We hear your mouth noise

but even our best
linguists can't follow your
facial orchestra how you say
one thing with your only
throat and another
with binocular
eyes. Sweet

unprepared neighbours where
is your biosphere where
your bodies were bred
to breath easy? What is
language good for if we can't tell
your scientists to leave before
the windstorm tears
the lineaments from the
earth? Bioengineering

is as natural to us as menopause
but you seem reluctant to bend
to the wind, though you shift
in the sun like heliotropic
plants. Instead of transfiguration
you terraform. Your temporary
constructs look like next generation's
homes as though any built thing
lasts a quintile here.

Your night machines
weave new
roads to nowhere you can
name yet.

We said 'dove-tail' and now they know

Earth has birds. In training
they taught us: avoid

metaphor, acronym, deflect
questions, use only words

that don't divulge secrets. *How did you
come here?* Say stars,

not ship. Say flight, not machine. Don't say
we 'beefed-up' 'base' 'security', 'hunted'

'wild' 'aves' in their 'backyard'. What is
'frost-bite' to people with no winter

or hands to freeze? 'Homesickness'
to those who never left? White lies feather

our tongues. Our children are born
full-strength like ungulates,

we say. Our skin is flight-
suit thick. We have no

weapons or weakness, no home
world to endanger.

Leaving was as easy as deprogramming

the settlement's OpSec; convincing security
doors to open and SmartEyes to close. I packed:

a hand-cranked tent and hammock,
the protein snacks kids still called

'space food,' a small hover sled
on its own WiFi, a shoulder-width

of un-ermine fur to warm me
when the suns set. I've been teaching myself

their language with tapes stolen
from the linguists' lab. I've been memorizing

star routes and storm patterns. My secret
penpal drew me a map and I drew

through the night to her. In the desert
we came together like stitches, like a pressure

seal closing around us. In our two-person
city, for two perfect weeks, we woke

tented in our never-before-seen
love and came home to our own conclusions.

Gastropod4Gastropod

I loved her the moment
I found her in the desert like a half-moon
snail dousing for molluscs, like a lost
drone lugging its mission home.

Why do all romantic metaphors sound predatory
in your language? Let me begin again.

Geopolitically, we were
toxic to each other the way
infection lusts for something
to ruin. We came asking
for estrangement.

Of course I loved her boiled
blister eyes, her simple mono-mouth.

I loved her face before and after
rearranging, how it knew the light
knew her.

Allodynia

If we'd known you
were coming we'd have sweetened
our laments and wished
for siblings. For eons
we radioed questions
into darkness and heard
your silence as extinction. Once here
you turned your city
gates stenotic, refused
all missives and messengers.

But when your young one
snuck into our desert
citadel and fell
in love with ours, we
offered her a joyful
dowry of augmentation, a bridal
crown of organs, a wedding
baptism of bound
wounds. Treated her
as our own. How could
we know you

don't heal in the night,
that you feel pain like
causation? We
wept devotion in our House of
Entrails, grieved
our knife quickness,
the harm done and undoable.

How allodynia blooms
even in the absence
of injury.

We forgave her family for their too-warm welcome and mine for their cold

We
arrived in their city cloaked in the same
hopeful fabric and though

I
was not the daughter-in-law they wanted
to knife, they took me with arms bent the right way.

Strange
how family shows acceptance
by fêting you for leaving.

Mine
heard my confessions and input
only danger, though I told

Them
often and gently that I crave
the night more than home.

They
buried my questions in the guest room
with the other unreliable objects, asked of

Me
nothing but a full-night's sleep, grieved
my absence and return in equal mounds.

Father
it is true, I have broken
curfew with the enemy;

43

I
have known their many
words for evening.

Love
held me between two inoperable
fingerprints and gave me everything she knew.

**Our training sims did not include a 'Star-Crossed Lovers'
scenario**

Later we'll ask, could
this have ended any way

other than way? A child
came home blinded by first

love and we leapt to ruin
our shirts with blood,

already wound-
eyed before we left.

The First War on Aeolia

Under siege we learned what your hands can do
when grafted with weapons, what holding

back hands us
back broken.
Don't think us

innocents: we had our inter-city combats,
our neighbourhood feuds, the scuffing
of black marks in the street where the dead
blew out like a tire. But before you

came, our conflicts
never came to
demolition, never came

for the load-bearing walls, for the vital veins, for the places
that can bleed out in the mouth of the city.

Abeona, Goddess of Outward Journeys, Hosts an AMA

I am this planet's smart(er-than thou)
black box, your impeachable preacher
and notetaker, so here goes for posterity! Future
analysts of best practices, documentaries of both
species and others still unregistered: Ask
Me Anything. I have unblinkable eyes and centuries
of back and forecasted data. I am more objective
than VAR; more observant than computer vision. I hold
every news release and lullaby, the blueprint of every
settlement, the outcomes of every
possible genetic combination, the dissemination
patterns of cultivated and wild seeds, every
blight, every avalanche, every injury. Ask me
which side struck first and hardest? What was seen
and unseen on the ground? On whose head
does blame fall like a guillotine or off the tongue?

PAIN LOG

Homebound

I got out of the hospital and came home
haunted. They misted with me

through the discharge station, clinging
to my hands in the cab. My doctors said

it was normal post-op
apparitions, just your everyday contagious

spooks, left like a forgotten IV port or surgical sponge,
a spectral infection hiding where I'd failed

to fumigate. Their prescription for banishment
was patience, hot baths, brisk walks with sharp

turns, pennies on the windowsill. At home, my stitches
undid themselves, fevers pet me

like a dog, my eyes opened
backwards. Sleep ghosted me

more than usual. Morning held the sheets down
but I woke most nights hovering in full

body palpitations, bent by the neck and elbow,
mouthing bacterial dust.

Floodplain

Tongue mossed over and algae blooming
my eyes, skeins

of pond scum knitting my hair. I'm at the bottom
of the lake, swallowing

the night's pill, zipping myself into a numb
bed under the current. The list

of things I've done
for my body is too long

to comb out and lay dry, so let
everything go to weeds: the shore walls

and the lake bed and the city's
flood plans

unweaving around me. The collective
nouns for this

are all liquid. A flood
of pain. A drowning

of pain. A pummelling,
even underwater.

When Drought Dries Your Eyes

A diving bell too heavy to lift cups the bed
every morning.   Small fires

you can't put out   wrestle your nerves
down to dust   near-ground turbulence rolling

dendrites like tumbleweeds.   A bulbar storm disinters
the atmosphere   sometimes squall, sometimes

fever, sometimes full force gale.   Diagnosis is half
superstition anyways   empiricism plus

hope plus the placebo effect   of naming
your enemy.   Have you tried sheathing

lightning in the soft
bellows of your cheek   gargling salt water

to read the residue?   These sudden seasons
of drought and drowning

are enough to steal
your balance on the backhand.

Your doctors keep trying
to set up an internal anemometer.   And you're out here

in the weather station   unsure if you should survey
the cloud ceiling or your tinder lungs.

The Illness Factory

In my fever, I laboured. I did the work
of diagnostics and daily maintenance, of pretending
to be well. I mapped out the best time of day
for every activity, rewired my motor

neurons to the house electrical so I could tense
the lights off, routed my tear ducts to the pipes
to flood the water tank. Every internal business
process optimized and streaming. But the truth

was I never *committed* to the role. I was a bad worker
of my own body. I rolled in late from the dayshift
at my *real life*, called in sick to my own sickbed,
spent too much on prescriptions and let profit

margins hover in the red. My safety
standards a hazard to everyone
in the vicinity. On shift, I was usually
one down and under

the influence. Hooked on the numb
cloud I'd float out on every night
and the reassurance of knowing
at least I was following doctor's orders.

I couldn't quit the business entirely but I shut down
the research wing. Fed up with not knowing
what the factory floor was making, I halted
all non-essential production. I called myself

into the office for a lecture on commitment
to the cause, gave myself a bad reference,
lay down in front of the machines I'd built
and begged them to dismantle me.

Things With No Home

Sparrows tumbled from my throat, which is to say
the surgery was a success.

There is room again
in my peritoneal cavity

for things with no home.
When they started dust bathing

between my costal cartilage, I learned
how to breath from the diaphragm

to launch an updraft, how to braid
sutures to seam

the scratch wounds. When they mistook
the sheathing on my nerves

for seed casings, I learned
how to tighten every lumen to pinpricks

too small for their preglossale
tongues, how to jut

my jaw so their feathers
don't catch in my teeth. Flocks

have been found nesting
in coal mines, eating stray

moths, unsure when to breed or sleep. The trick
is to coax them out

into a dark room so they don't notice
they're leaving you.

Apicoectomy

He turns your chest
into a surgical tray, picking
drills and sickle probes
out of the line-up. You're numbed

down on lidocaine and the doll-like
patience of being your own
operating table, dress too short to be
hung from this angle, eyes

rolled back so you can watch
the news on the ceiling TV, pillowing
his knuckles with your ice cheeks
so he can carve the perfect bite. He goes in

through the flesh and it's a mouthful
of stitches and bloody teeth, a bone graft
if you're unlucky. Each time
in the chair, the swollen

hope that everything
that ails you comes down to an apex
infection humming under
your gums, furrows of sulking

fever, the concert of canaries
that is your immune system.

Evoked Potential

She's the only person in the hospital
who runs these tests. The neuro-diagnostics.

Every day she swabs scalps with alcohol, tapes
electrodes to limbs, cleans

conducting gel out of hair. Checking
the latency between stimulus

and response: a visual aberration,
a loud click, electrical pulses

at the wrist and knees. She sees
the guesswork patients, the ones

who have spent years arguing *something*
is eating me with narrow teeth. Sometimes

they scream, but the response doesn't always
indicate a measurable problem. It's not

that they overreact. But their signal-to-noise ratio
is uneven. Bracing so hard they feel

future pain gripped in their fists. At home
she cups her wife's head

with hands rashed from the insides
of gloves; coats her skin in cream

before bed. She isn't a doctor
or a priest. All she can test is if her patient's

amplitude and spectral sensitivity is within
normal range; if they're walking

around at a sensory disadvantage,
axons left hanging, blinking quietly.

Phase Change

Halfway up the climbing
wall, rising heat is reverse
chalk dusting my fingers
til I slip. I lose
speech first and whatever
neural impulse commands
basic ambulation. How
embarrassing: becoming
vapour in public. Auto-
immune disease is more
common at higher
latitudes where sunlight is less
dense; something about
non-genomic immunomodulatory

function. This is not
a metaphor, but a caution
for your future children, suntanning
in the womb. I'm from one
of the coldest cities
in the world and heat
kneels me. In an air-
conditioned gym, I can squat
100 pounds but carrying
groceries home in summer
sweat leaves me
shambling. It's a kind
of disassociation;
my body separates
from my soul

under duress. I used to think
of myself as without
limits, but I'm learning
my combustion
point, the red line beyond
which I cannot be held
responsible. My bellwether is sudden
clumsiness; nerves
so blunted I burn
a layer of skin leaning
into the oven.

The Small Animal

In the moment between morning
and pain I forget my body
is an engine and lie
waiting for an external
force to drive me up and into the day's
ache. There's usually enough

volts in the pins
and needles in my hands to take
a small animal down
but on a bad day I can't power
my own eyelids open. No one believes

me except my osteopath, who sees
if not the cause, than
at least the ways my muscles
twist around the problem. With my head

in her hands she triggers
small buttons for partial
release. I once saw
an eagle pick a baby
rabbit up by the neck. I am kind

of like that, limp on her table.
My doctors tell me it's a kind
of haunting. Old infections
sulking in corners. All the symptoms

I only recognize because my mother
had them, unnamed
and badly treated. I tell them
it's the old Yiddish curse:

you will appear
healthy but secretly writhe.

Ritual for Removing 'Opioid-Seeking' From Your File

Sit sweet-mouthed in the doctor's office in your best
'reliable witness' costume, ghosts braiding your hair. Appear
ill but not in need. Competent but not complicated. Well-

spoken but not too prepared. Memorize side effects. Dress neatly.
Smooth your skirt. Still your face. Controlled
substances means you can't cry if she says 'no.' Good

girls don't want it this bad so you don't tell her
about the haunting. How they find you
crumpled on your own doorstep trying to get your shaking

keys through the door. How they paint you into bed, legs
calved in metal. You don't tell her about the days spent unhooking
yourself from well-meant prescriptions. But what do you know

better than your own body. Your own
fever. Your own hands on your brow. Your own
stealth. Your own storms. Your own

sorrow. Your own safety. Your own pain. Your own
falls. Your own fault. Your own fault. Your own body
and it's haunted halls and absentee owner.

Affinity for Falling

Once a stranger's shoulder caught mine and I slid
down the escalator taking the brunt of the fall on my right
butt cheek and an elbow that will flicker for years, radial

nerve falling numb mid exam, bloody knees I won't notice
'til I'm halfway to work and see the whole metro car staring.
Once my handlebars twisted and I came down hard, palms

praying on the road, nose inches from broken. Once I spent
a five-hour flight tensed on the bathroom floor, unsure
if it was flu or a miscommunication in my immune system's

well-armed defense, waiting for the safe landing I couldn't trust
my own body to carry off. Once cocky at the gym, testing angled
push-ups on a balance ball, something cranked in my rhomboid

flipped me to the ground. As a kid I dreamed of somersaulting
down the staircase, jumping off the upstairs porch like the cat
I once catapulted into the garden trying to shovel snow. Now

there are days when my body trips me just to make me lie
down, when I can't make it safely past a flight of stairs, when it's better
to take me down by the knees then let me out in the world, falling hard
                                                        over everything.

All Our Unreasonable Fears

Good morning to the easily
shaken. To the bad

sleepers. To my fellow
shallow breathers working half

a lung. To my sisters quick to climb
the mountain of worst-

case scenarios. To everyone barely
keeping a lid on their interior

boiling. To all our unreasonable
fears blooming in a litany

of what-ifs. Let's comfort ourselves
by calculating the probability

of the year's disasters, the vectors
of disease tessering

near us. Here, where everyone
judges our attention

span by how still we keep, I'll be
the queen of leaping

first, logic following
me like a dog.

Acknowledgements

Prior versions of poems in this collection have appeared in *13: New Collected Poems from LGBTQI2S Writers* (League of Canadian Poets), *antilang, Apparition Lit, Augur Magazine, Bloodbath Literary Zine, Carte Blanche, Contemporary Verse 2, Cosmonauts Avenue, Entropy Magazine, Feels Zine, Grain Magazine, Malahat Review, Minola Review, small poems for the masses, Strange Horizons, The Fiddlehead, The L4 Society Zine, The Puritan, Watch Your Head,* and *What Stops You What Carries On.*

Many poems from the "Pain Log" sections appeared in the chapbook *Remitting* (Baseline Press, 2019), which won the 2020 bpNichol Award.

"Abeona, Goddess of Outward Journeys, pilots the interstellar ark" was nominated for a 2020 Rhysling Award by *Apparition Lit.*

"Lumbar Puncture" was a finalist for *Anesthesiology's* 2020 Letheon Prize.

With thanks to the Ontario Arts Council, the Toronto Arts Council, the Banff Centre for Arts and Creativity, Artscape Gibraltar Point, and the incredible teams at Palimpsest Press, Anstruther Books, and Baseline Press.

Photo by Jen Allison

NISA MALLI is a writer and a researcher, born in Winnipeg and currently living in Toronto. She holds a BFA in Creative Writing from the University of Victoria and has completed residencies at the Banff Centre and Artscape Gibraltar Point. Her first chapbook, *Remitting* (Baseline Press, 2019) won the bpNichol Prize. *Allodynia* is her first full-length book.